EMMANUEL JOSEPH

Beyond the Binary, A Philosophical and Historical Exploration of Technological Evolution

Copyright © 2025 by Emmanuel Joseph

All rights reserved. No part of this publication may be reproduced, stored or transmitted in any form or by any means, electronic, mechanical, photocopying, recording, scanning, or otherwise without written permission from the publisher. It is illegal to copy this book, post it to a website, or distribute it by any other means without permission.

First edition

This book was professionally typeset on Reedsy.
Find out more at reedsy.com

Contents

1	Chapter 1: The Dawn of Human Ingenuity	1
2	Chapter 2: The Age of Enlightenment and Industrial…	3
3	Chapter 3: The Digital Age and the Rise of Computers	5
4	Chapter 4: The Information Revolution and the Birth of the…	7
5	Chapter 5: The Age of Artificial Intelligence	9
6	Chapter 6: The Quantum Leap: Exploring Quantum Computing	11
7	Chapter 7: The Internet of Things and Smart Technologies	13
8	Chapter 8: Biotechnology and the Future of Medicine	15
9	Chapter 9: The Ethical Implications of Technological…	17
10	Chapter 10: The Role of Philosophy in Technological…	19
11	Chapter 11: The Future of Human-Machine Collaboration	22
12	Chapter 12: The Role of Education in Technological…	24
13	Chapter 13: The Intersection of Art and Technology	26
14	Chapter 14: Space Exploration and the New Frontier	28
15	Chapter 15: The Future of Technological Evolution	30

1

Chapter 1: The Dawn of Human Ingenuity

The story of human technological evolution begins with our earliest ancestors, who fashioned tools from stone to meet their basic needs. These primitive implements, although simple, marked a significant departure from the unadorned life of other animals. With each sharpened flint and carved bone, humanity took steps towards greater control over their environment. This primal ingenuity laid the foundation for future innovations, setting the stage for more complex creations.

Moving forward from the Stone Age, the discovery of metallurgy revolutionized human societies. The ability to mold and manipulate metals like copper and bronze paved the way for advanced agricultural tools and weapons. This newfound expertise not only increased efficiency in everyday tasks but also spurred social and economic transformations. The significance of these early advancements cannot be overstated, as they laid the groundwork for the technological revolutions that followed.

As human societies grew more complex, so too did their technological pursuits. The invention of the wheel, for instance, transformed transportation and trade, enabling the movement of goods and people across vast distances. This innovation facilitated cultural exchange and the spread of ideas, knitting together distant communities into a cohesive web of human endeavor. These early breakthroughs were more than mere tools; they were catalysts for progress, driving humanity ever forward.

BEYOND THE BINARY, A PHILOSOPHICAL AND HISTORICAL EXPLORATION OF TECHNOLOGICAL EVOLUTION

By tracing the origins of human ingenuity, we uncover the roots of our relentless drive to innovate. From the earliest flint tools to the complex machinery of ancient civilizations, our ancestors demonstrated an innate curiosity and resourcefulness. This unyielding pursuit of knowledge and mastery over the natural world set the stage for the technological marvels that define our modern age.

2

Chapter 2: The Age of Enlightenment and Industrial Revolution

The Age of Enlightenment heralded a new era of intellectual fervor and scientific discovery. Philosophers and thinkers like Isaac Newton, John Locke, and Voltaire championed the power of reason and empirical evidence. This shift in thinking laid the groundwork for the technological advancements that would follow, as people began to question long-held beliefs and seek out new truths. The Enlightenment was not just an intellectual movement; it was a catalyst for profound technological change.

The Industrial Revolution, which began in the late 18th century, was a direct consequence of Enlightenment thinking. This period saw the birth of mechanized production and the rise of factories, transforming societies from agrarian economies to industrial powerhouses. Innovations such as the steam engine, spinning jenny, and power loom revolutionized manufacturing processes, increasing productivity and efficiency. The Industrial Revolution not only reshaped economies but also altered the fabric of everyday life.

As cities grew and industries flourished, the demand for labor skyrocketed, leading to significant social changes. Urbanization brought people from rural areas to burgeoning metropolises, creating diverse and dynamic communities. The rapid pace of technological advancement during this period was both exhilarating and challenging, as societies grappled with the implications of industrialization. The Industrial Revolution was a time of unprecedented growth and change, as humanity harnessed the power of machines to shape the world.

The legacy of the Enlightenment and Industrial Revolution is still evident today. The principles of reason, empirical evidence, and technological innovation continue to drive progress in various fields. By understanding the historical context and philosophical underpinnings of these transformative periods, we gain a deeper appreciation for the technological advancements that define our modern world. The Age of Enlightenment and Industrial Revolution were not just epochs of change; they were the crucibles in which the future was forged.

3

Chapter 3: The Digital Age and the Rise of Computers

The 20th century ushered in the Digital Age, a period marked by rapid advancements in computing and information technology. The development of electronic computers revolutionized the way we process, store, and transmit information. Early pioneers like Alan Turing, John von Neumann, and Grace Hopper laid the groundwork for modern computing, developing foundational concepts and architectures that continue to influence technology today.

The invention of the transistor in 1947 by John Bardeen, Walter Brattain, and William Shockley was a pivotal moment in the history of technology. This tiny semiconductor device enabled the creation of smaller, faster, and more efficient computers, paving the way for the microelectronics revolution. The subsequent development of integrated circuits and microprocessors further accelerated the pace of technological progress, leading to the proliferation of personal computers and digital devices.

The rise of the Internet in the late 20th century transformed the world in ways that were previously unimaginable. This global network of interconnected computers facilitated the rapid exchange of information, breaking down geographical barriers and fostering unprecedented levels of collaboration and communication. The Internet revolutionized industries, from commerce and entertainment to education and healthcare, fundamentally altering the way we live and work.

As we navigate the complexities of the Digital Age, it is essential to recognize the profound impact of computing technology on our society. The rise of computers has not only revolutionized industries and economies but also reshaped our daily lives. By understanding the historical and philosophical context of these technological advancements, we can better appreciate the profound changes that have shaped our world and continue to drive progress in the 21st century.

4

Chapter 4: The Information Revolution and the Birth of the Internet

The Information Revolution, which began in the latter half of the 20th century, was characterized by the rapid proliferation of digital technologies and the exponential growth of information. The development of computer networks and the subsequent rise of the Internet transformed the way we access, share, and consume information. This period of unprecedented technological change marked a fundamental shift in how we interact with the world around us.

The origins of the Internet can be traced back to the 1960s when researchers at the Advanced Research Projects Agency (ARPA) developed the ARPANET, the precursor to the modern Internet. This early network connected a small number of research institutions, allowing scientists to share data and collaborate on projects in real time. The success of ARPANET demonstrated the potential of computer networks and laid the foundation for the global Internet.

The 1990s saw the commercialization of the Internet and the rise of the World Wide Web, developed by British scientist Tim Berners-Lee. The Web revolutionized the way we access and share information, making it possible for anyone with an Internet connection to publish and consume content. This democratization of information had far-reaching implications, enabling the rise of e-commerce, social media, and online education, among other innovations.

As we reflect on the Information Revolution and the birth of the Internet, it is important to consider the philosophical and ethical implications of these technological advancements. The digital age has brought about unprecedented levels of connectivity and access to information, but it has also raised questions about privacy, security, and the digital divide. By understanding the historical context and philosophical underpinnings of the Information Revolution, we can better navigate the challenges and opportunities of the digital age.

5

Chapter 5: The Age of Artificial Intelligence

The development of artificial intelligence (AI) represents one of the most significant technological advancements of the 21st century. AI, which encompasses a range of technologies designed to mimic human intelligence, has the potential to transform various aspects of our lives. From self-driving cars and virtual assistants to advanced medical diagnostics and predictive analytics, AI is poised to revolutionize industries and reshape our society.

The roots of AI can be traced back to the mid-20th century when researchers like Alan Turing and John McCarthy began to explore the possibility of creating machines that could think and learn like humans. The development of machine learning algorithms and neural networks in the latter half of the 20th century paved the way for the advanced AI systems we see today. These technologies have enabled machines to analyze vast amounts of data, identify patterns, and make decisions with remarkable accuracy.

As AI continues to evolve, it raises important philosophical and ethical questions about the nature of intelligence, autonomy, and the role of technology in our lives. The potential benefits of AI are immense, but so too are the risks and challenges. Issues such as bias in AI algorithms, the impact of automation on employment, and the ethical implications of autonomous systems must be carefully considered as we navigate the AI revolution.

The Age of Artificial Intelligence represents a new frontier in technological evolution, one that holds great promise and significant challenges. By understanding the historical context and philosophical underpinnings of AI, we can better appreciate its potential impact on our society and make informed decisions about its development and deployment. The future of AI is still unfolding, and it is up to us to shape it in ways that align with our values and aspirations.

6

Chapter 6: The Quantum Leap: Exploring Quantum Computing

Quantum computing represents a paradigm shift in the field of computer science, offering the potential to solve complex problems that are currently beyond the reach of classical computers. Unlike traditional computers, which use bits to represent information as 0s and 1s, quantum computers use quantum bits or qubits, which can exist in multiple states simultaneously. This unique property, known as superposition, enables quantum computers to process information at unprecedented speeds.

The development of quantum computing has its roots in the early 20th century when physicists like Niels Bohr and Albert Einstein began to explore the strange and counterintuitive properties of quantum mechanics. Theoretical work by scientists such as Richard Feynman and David Deutsch in the latter half of the century laid the groundwork for practical quantum computing. Today, researchers are working to build scalable quantum computers that can tackle problems in fields ranging from cryptography and materials science to artificial intelligence and climate modeling.

The potential applications of quantum computing are vast and transformative. For example, quantum computers could revolutionize drug discovery by simulating the behavior of complex molecules at the quantum level, enabling researchers to design new medications with unprecedented precision. In the field of cryptography, quantum computers could break current encryption schemes, necessitating the development of new, quantum-resistant security protocols. The implications of quantum computing extend far beyond the realm of technology, touching on philosophical questions about the nature of reality and the limits of human knowledge.

As researchers continue to push the boundaries of quantum computing, they must also grapple with the ethical and societal implications of this powerful technology. Questions about access, equity, and the potential for misuse are critical considerations as we move toward a future shaped by quantum computing. By understanding the historical context and philosophical underpinnings of this technological revolution, we can better navigate the challenges and opportunities it presents. The quantum leap represents not just a technological advancement, but a profound shift in our understanding of the universe and our place within it.

7

Chapter 7: The Internet of Things and Smart Technologies

The Internet of Things (IoT) refers to the network of interconnected devices that communicate and exchange data with each other. This technological paradigm shift has transformed various aspects of our daily lives, from smart homes and wearable fitness trackers to industrial automation and connected transportation systems. The proliferation of IoT devices has created a seamless web of technology that enhances efficiency, convenience, and connectivity.

The concept of IoT has its roots in the early 21st century when the convergence of wireless communication, sensor technology, and data analytics enabled the development of smart devices. These devices, embedded with sensors and equipped with internet connectivity, can collect and transmit data in real time. This ability to gather and analyze vast amounts of data has opened up new possibilities for innovation and optimization across various sectors.

One of the most significant impacts of IoT is in the realm of smart cities. By integrating IoT technologies into urban infrastructure, cities can optimize resource management, improve public services, and enhance the quality of life for their residents. From smart traffic lights that reduce congestion to environmental sensors that monitor air quality, IoT is transforming the way we live and interact with our environment. However, the widespread adoption of IoT also raises important questions about privacy, security, and the ethical use of data.

As we continue to embrace IoT and smart technologies, it is crucial to consider the broader implications of this interconnected world. The potential benefits of IoT are immense, but so too are the risks and challenges. By understanding the historical context and philosophical underpinnings of IoT, we can better navigate the opportunities and pitfalls of this technological revolution. The Internet of Things represents a new era of connectivity and innovation, one that has the power to reshape our society and redefine the boundaries of what is possible.

8

Chapter 8: Biotechnology and the Future of Medicine

Biotechnology represents a convergence of biology and technology that has the potential to revolutionize the field of medicine. By harnessing the power of genetic engineering, biopharmaceuticals, and regenerative medicine, biotechnology offers new possibilities for diagnosing, treating, and preventing diseases. The advancements in this field have not only extended human life expectancy but also improved the quality of life for millions of people worldwide.

The origins of biotechnology can be traced back to the discovery of the structure of DNA by James Watson and Francis Crick in 1953. This groundbreaking discovery paved the way for genetic engineering and the development of recombinant DNA technology. The subsequent advent of the Human Genome Project in the 1990s further accelerated the pace of biotechnological advancements, providing researchers with a comprehensive map of the human genome. This knowledge has been instrumental in developing targeted therapies and personalized medicine.

One of the most promising areas of biotechnology is regenerative medicine, which aims to repair or replace damaged tissues and organs using stem cells and tissue engineering techniques. Advances in this field have led to the development of innovative treatments for conditions such as spinal cord injuries, heart disease, and diabetes. Additionally, biopharmaceuticals, which include drugs produced using living organisms, have revolutionized the treatment of various diseases, from cancer to autoimmune disorders.

As biotechnology continues to advance, it raises important ethical and philosophical questions about the nature of life, the limits of human intervention, and the potential consequences of manipulating biological systems. The benefits of biotechnology are immense, but so too are the risks and challenges. By understanding the historical context and philosophical underpinnings of this field, we can better navigate the opportunities and pitfalls of this technological revolution. The future of medicine lies at the intersection of biology and technology, offering new possibilities for improving human health and well-being.

9

Chapter 9: The Ethical Implications of Technological Advancements

The rapid pace of technological advancements has brought about profound changes in various aspects of our lives, raising important ethical and philosophical questions. As we navigate the complexities of the digital age, it is crucial to consider the broader implications of these innovations. The ethical challenges posed by technologies such as artificial intelligence, biotechnology, and quantum computing require careful consideration and thoughtful deliberation.

One of the central ethical concerns in the age of technology is the issue of privacy. The proliferation of digital devices and the collection of vast amounts of data have raised questions about the protection of personal information and the potential for misuse. Ensuring that data is collected, stored, and used in a manner that respects individual privacy and autonomy is a critical challenge in the digital age. Additionally, the ethical implications of surveillance technologies and the potential for abuse by governments and corporations must be carefully examined.

Another significant ethical challenge is the issue of equity and access. As technological advancements continue to reshape various aspects of society, it is essential to ensure that the benefits of these innovations are equitably distributed. Addressing the digital divide and ensuring access to technology for underserved populations are critical considerations in the pursuit of a just and inclusive technological future. Moreover, the impact of automation and artificial intelligence on employment and the potential for job displacement require careful consideration and proactive measures to mitigate adverse effects.

The ethical implications of technological advancements also extend to the broader questions of human autonomy and agency. As we develop increasingly sophisticated AI systems and autonomous technologies, it is essential to consider the potential consequences for individual autonomy and decision-making. Ensuring that technology serves to enhance rather than diminish human agency is a critical ethical consideration. By grappling with these ethical challenges, we can better navigate the complexities of the digital age and ensure that technological advancements align with our values and aspirations.

10

Chapter 10: The Role of Philosophy in Technological Evolution

Philosophy has played a crucial role in shaping our understanding of technological evolution and its implications for society. From the early thinkers of the Enlightenment to contemporary philosophers, the examination of the ethical, epistemological, and metaphysical dimensions of technology has provided valuable insights into the nature of technological progress. By engaging with philosophical inquiry, we can develop a deeper understanding of the broader implications of technological advancements and navigate the complexities of the digital age.

One of the central themes in the philosophy of technology is the relationship between humans and machines. Philosophers such as Martin Heidegger and Jacques Ellul have explored the ways in which technology shapes our perception of the world and our interactions with it. Heidegger's concept of "enframing" suggests that technology imposes a particular way of understanding and engaging with reality, influencing our thoughts and actions. By critically examining the ways in which technology shapes our worldview, we can develop a more nuanced understanding of its impact on society.

Another important area of philosophical inquiry is the ethics of technology. Philosophers such as Hans Jonas and John Rawls have explored the ethical implications of technological advancements and the responsibilities of individuals and societies in the face of these changes. Jonas's principle of responsibility emphasizes the need to consider the long-term consequences of technological innovations and to act with caution and foresight. Rawls's theory of justice provides a framework for ensuring that the benefits of technology are distributed equitably and that the rights and interests of all individuals are respected.

The epistemological dimensions of technology also warrant careful consideration. The development of artificial intelligence and machine learning raises questions about the nature of knowledge and the limits of human understanding. Philosophers such as Hubert Dreyfus and Luciano Floridi have explored the ways in which AI challenges traditional notions of knowledge and cognition. By engaging with these philosophical questions, we can develop a more comprehensive understanding of the implications of AI and other advanced technologies.

The epistemological dimensions of technology also warrant careful consideration. The development of artificial intelligence and machine learning raises questions about the nature of knowledge and the limits of human understanding. Philosophers such as Hubert Dreyfus and Luciano Floridi have explored the ways in which AI challenges traditional notions of knowledge and cognition. By engaging with these philosophical questions, we can develop a more comprehensive understanding of the implications of AI and other advanced technologies.

Another important aspect of the philosophy of technology is the examination of the relationship between technology and society. The work of philosophers such as Langdon Winner and Andrew Feenberg has highlighted the ways in which technology shapes social structures and power dynamics. Winner's concept of "technological determinism" suggests that technological development follows its own logic, independent of social and political influences. Feenberg, on the other hand, argues for a more nuanced view, emphasizing the role of human agency in shaping technological outcomes.

The exploration of the philosophical dimensions of technology provides valuable insights into the broader implications of technological evolution.

By critically examining the ethical, epistemological, and social dimensions of technology, we can develop a more holistic understanding of its impact on society. Engaging with philosophical inquiry allows us to navigate the complexities of the digital age with greater clarity and foresight, ensuring that technological advancements align with our values and aspirations.

11

Chapter 11: The Future of Human-Machine Collaboration

As technology continues to evolve, the collaboration between humans and machines is becoming increasingly sophisticated. The integration of artificial intelligence, robotics, and automation into various aspects of our lives has the potential to enhance human capabilities and improve efficiency. However, this collaboration also raises important questions about the nature of work, the role of human expertise, and the ethical implications of automation.

One of the most promising areas of human-machine collaboration is in the field of healthcare. The use of AI and robotics in medical diagnostics, surgery, and patient care has the potential to revolutionize the practice of medicine. For example, AI algorithms can analyze vast amounts of medical data to identify patterns and make accurate diagnoses, while robotic surgical systems can perform minimally invasive procedures with precision and accuracy. These technologies have the potential to improve patient outcomes and reduce the burden on healthcare professionals.

Another important area of human-machine collaboration is in the workplace. Automation and AI technologies can augment human capabilities, enabling workers to perform tasks more efficiently and safely. For example, in manufacturing, robots can handle repetitive and physically demanding

CHAPTER 11: THE FUTURE OF HUMAN-MACHINE COLLABORATION

tasks, allowing human workers to focus on more complex and creative aspects of production. However, the integration of automation into the workplace also raises questions about the future of employment and the potential displacement of workers. Addressing these challenges requires thoughtful consideration and proactive measures to ensure that the benefits of automation are equitably distributed.

The future of human-machine collaboration holds great promise, but it also requires careful navigation of the ethical, social, and economic implications. By understanding the historical context and philosophical underpinnings of this collaboration, we can better appreciate its potential impact and develop strategies to ensure that it aligns with our values and aspirations. The integration of human and machine capabilities represents a new frontier in technological evolution, one that has the power to transform various aspects of our lives.

12

Chapter 12: The Role of Education in Technological Advancement

Education plays a crucial role in shaping the future of technological advancement. By equipping individuals with the knowledge and skills needed to navigate the complexities of the digital age, education can empower people to become active participants in technological innovation. The rapid pace of technological change necessitates a rethinking of traditional educational models and the development of new approaches to learning.

One of the key challenges in education is preparing students for a future that is increasingly shaped by technology. This requires a focus on developing not only technical skills but also critical thinking, creativity, and adaptability. Integrating technology into the classroom can enhance learning experiences and provide students with hands-on opportunities to explore and experiment with new tools and concepts. By fostering a culture of innovation and inquiry, education can empower individuals to become lifelong learners and active contributors to technological advancement.

Another important aspect of education is ensuring equitable access to technology and learning opportunities. Addressing the digital divide and providing underserved populations with access to quality education and digital resources is critical in the pursuit of a just and inclusive technological future.

CHAPTER 12: THE ROLE OF EDUCATION IN TECHNOLOGICAL...

This requires investment in infrastructure, teacher training, and community outreach programs to bridge the gap and ensure that all individuals have the opportunity to benefit from technological advancements.

The role of education in technological advancement extends beyond the classroom. Lifelong learning and professional development are essential in a world where technological change is constant. By providing individuals with opportunities to update their skills and stay current with technological trends, education can support workforce adaptability and resilience. The future of education is inextricably linked to the future of technology, and by understanding the historical and philosophical context, we can better navigate the challenges and opportunities of this dynamic relationship.

13

Chapter 13: The Intersection of Art and Technology

The intersection of art and technology is a dynamic and evolving space that has the potential to push the boundaries of creative expression and innovation. From digital art and virtual reality installations to AI-generated music and interactive performances, the fusion of art and technology is opening up new possibilities for artists and audiences alike. This convergence challenges traditional notions of art and invites us to explore the ways in which technology can enhance and transform the creative process.

One of the most exciting developments in this space is the use of artificial intelligence in the creation of art. AI algorithms can analyze vast amounts of data, identify patterns, and generate original works of art that challenge our understanding of creativity and authorship. For example, AI-generated paintings and music compositions have been exhibited in galleries and performed in concert halls, sparking conversations about the role of technology in the creative process. These works raise important questions about the nature of creativity, the definition of art, and the relationship between human and machine.

Virtual reality (VR) and augmented reality (AR) technologies are also transforming the way we experience and interact with art. VR and AR installations can create immersive and interactive environments that engage

CHAPTER 13: THE INTERSECTION OF ART AND TECHNOLOGY

audiences in new and exciting ways. These technologies enable artists to experiment with spatial dimensions, narrative structures, and sensory experiences, pushing the boundaries of traditional art forms. The use of VR and AR in art invites us to reconsider the relationship between the viewer and the artwork, blurring the lines between reality and imagination.

The intersection of art and technology also has important implications for cultural preservation and accessibility. Digital technologies can be used to document, preserve, and share cultural heritage, making it accessible to a global audience. For example, 3D scanning and printing technologies can create detailed replicas of historical artifacts, allowing researchers and the public to explore and study them in new ways. Additionally, online platforms and digital archives can provide access to artworks and cultural resources that were previously limited by geographical and physical constraints.

By exploring the intersection of art and technology, we can gain a deeper appreciation for the ways in which these fields can inform and inspire each other. The fusion of art and technology is not just about creating new tools or techniques; it is about reimagining the possibilities of human expression and creativity. By understanding the historical and philosophical context of this convergence, we can better appreciate its potential impact and navigate the challenges and opportunities it presents.

14

Chapter 14: Space Exploration and the New Frontier

Space exploration represents one of the most ambitious and awe-inspiring technological endeavors of humanity. From the early days of rocketry to the modern era of space travel, the quest to explore the cosmos has driven technological innovation and expanded our understanding of the universe. The achievements of space exploration, from landing on the moon to sending probes to distant planets, have captured the imagination of people around the world and inspired generations of scientists and engineers.

The origins of space exploration can be traced back to the mid-20th century when the United States and the Soviet Union engaged in a race to conquer the final frontier. The launch of Sputnik 1, the first artificial satellite, by the Soviet Union in 1957 marked the beginning of the space age. This milestone was followed by a series of historic achievements, including the first human spaceflight by Yuri Gagarin in 1961 and the Apollo 11 moon landing in 1969. These early successes demonstrated the potential of space exploration and set the stage for future missions.

In recent years, space exploration has entered a new era characterized by increased international collaboration and the involvement of private companies. Organizations such as NASA, ESA, and SpaceX are pushing the boundaries of what is possible, developing advanced spacecraft and

CHAPTER 14: SPACE EXPLORATION AND THE NEW FRONTIER

technologies to explore the moon, Mars, and beyond. The ambitious goal of establishing a sustainable human presence on other planets has driven advancements in fields such as robotics, materials science, and life support systems. These efforts are not only expanding our knowledge of the universe but also inspiring new generations to dream big and pursue careers in science and engineering.

The future of space exploration holds great promise and significant challenges. The quest to explore the cosmos raises important questions about the ethics of space colonization, the potential for extraterrestrial life, and the role of humanity in the universe. By understanding the historical context and philosophical underpinnings of space exploration, we can better appreciate its impact on society and navigate the complexities of this new frontier. The journey to the stars is not just a technological endeavor; it is a profound exploration of our place in the cosmos.

15

Chapter 15: The Future of Technological Evolution

As we look to the future, it is clear that technological evolution will continue to shape and define our world in profound ways. Emerging technologies such as artificial intelligence, quantum computing, biotechnology, and space exploration hold the potential to revolutionize various aspects of our lives and drive progress in ways that are currently unimaginable. The future of technological evolution is a dynamic and ever-changing landscape, filled with both opportunities and challenges.

One of the key drivers of future technological evolution is the continued advancement of artificial intelligence. AI has the potential to transform industries, improve healthcare, and address complex global challenges. The development of more sophisticated AI systems, capable of learning and adapting in real time, will enable new applications and innovations. However, the ethical implications of AI, including issues of bias, transparency, and accountability, must be carefully considered to ensure that this technology is developed and deployed responsibly.

Another important area of future technological evolution is the convergence of biotechnology and medicine. Advances in genetic engineering, personalized medicine, and regenerative therapies hold the potential to revolutionize healthcare and improve the quality of life for millions of people.

CHAPTER 15: THE FUTURE OF TECHNOLOGICAL EVOLUTION

The ability to edit genes, develop targeted therapies, and regenerate damaged tissues opens up new possibilities for treating diseases and extending human longevity. However, the ethical and societal implications of these technologies must be carefully examined to ensure that they are used in ways that align with our values and principles.

The future of technological evolution also holds exciting possibilities for space exploration and the quest to explore the cosmos. The development of advanced propulsion systems, life support technologies, and sustainable habitats will enable humans to venture further into space and establish a presence on other planets. These advancements will not only expand our understanding of the universe but also inspire new generations to dream big and pursue careers in science and engineering.

As we navigate the future of technological evolution, it is essential to engage in thoughtful and informed discussions about the ethical, social, and philosophical implications of emerging technologies. By understanding the historical context and philosophical underpinnings of technological progress, we can better appreciate its impact on society and make informed decisions about its development and deployment. The future of technological evolution is filled with possibilities, and it is up to us to shape it in ways that align with our values and aspirations.

In **"Beyond the Binary: A Philosophical and Historical Exploration of Technological Evolution,"** embark on a captivating journey through the history of technology and its profound impact on human society. From the dawn of human ingenuity and the creation of early tools to the rise of artificial intelligence and quantum computing, this book delves into the key milestones that have shaped our technological landscape.

Each chapter weaves together historical events, philosophical insights, and ethical considerations, offering a comprehensive exploration of how technology has evolved and transformed our world. Discover the pivotal moments in the Age of Enlightenment and Industrial Revolution, the revolutionary advancements of the Digital Age and the Internet, and the groundbreaking developments in biotechnology and space exploration.

As we look toward the future, "Beyond the Binary" examines the challenges and opportunities presented by emerging technologies. The book invites readers to reflect on the ethical implications of technological advancements, the role of education in fostering innovation, and the dynamic interplay between art and technology. By understanding the historical and philosophical context of technological evolution, readers are equipped to navigate the complexities of the digital age with greater clarity and foresight.

"Beyond the Binary" is a thought-provoking exploration of humanity's relentless drive to innovate and the profound impact of technology on our lives. This book is a must-read for anyone interested in the intersection of technology, philosophy, and history, and offers valuable insights into the future of human-machine collaboration and the ever-evolving technological frontier.

www.ingramcontent.com/pod-product-compliance
Lightning Source LLC
LaVergne TN
LVHW020500080526
838202LV00057B/6066